The Crossing Point of Our Lives

The Crossing Point of Our Lives

A Gathering of Christian Poems

JOHN J. BRUGALETTA

RESOURCE *Publications* • Eugene, Oregon

THE CROSSING POINT OF OUR LIVES
A Gathering of Christian Poems

Copyright © 2022 John J. Brugaletta. All rights reserved. Except for brief quotations in critical publications or reviews, no part of this book may be reproduced in any manner without prior written permission from the publisher. Write: Permissions, Wipf and Stock Publishers, 199 W. 8th Ave., Suite 3, Eugene, OR 97401.

Resource Publications
An Imprint of Wipf and Stock Publishers
199 W. 8th Ave., Suite 3
Eugene, OR 97401

www.wipfandstock.com

PAPERBACK ISBN: 978-1-6667-3655-7
HARDCOVER ISBN: 978-1-6667-9505-9
EBOOK ISBN: 978-1-6667-9506-6

JANUARY 7, 2022 11:51 AM

For John Travis Brugaletta
brilliant man
excellent son
good friend

Contents

Acknowledgments | ix

TALKING TO GOD
The potter | 3
Messiah | 4
Nothing In Excess | 5
His Foolish Aim | 6
Prayer For Pain | 7
For The Church Universal | 8
Is There only one? | 9

DRAMATIC MONOLOGUES
Malchus | 13
The Magi | 14
Gabriel | 15
Seen From A Caboose | 16
Simon Of Cyrene | 17
Parable For Our Time | 18
A Pivot Point | 19
The Business Of Repentance | 20
Fantastic Sins | 21
Joses | 22

A MISCELLANY

Unseen, Dr. Johnson Hears Praise | 25
Discounting Truths | 26
The Beginning And The End | 27
In Quest Of The Holy Grail | 29
Our Road | 30
An Old Story | 31
Fingerprints | 32
Dedications | 33
Easter | 34
Easter II | 35
Easter Sunday | 36
Sweet Are The Uses… | 37
Unworthy | 38
Looking For Heaven | 39
A Change For The Better | 40
Praying Or Playing? | 41
At The Crucial Point | 42
Civilization | 43

THE PELEGRIN PAPERS: A SET OF NARRATIVES

1. Sir Pelegrin | 47
2. Young Pelegrin | 53
3. The Sheriff | 55
4. The Drunkard Priest | 57
5. The Bishop | 61
6. Sir Pelegrin's Granddaughter | 63
7. The Boy At The Bishop's Palace | 66

Acknowledgments

The poems below were previously published in the journals indicated, some of them in a slightly different form.

The Penwood Review	"The Potter"
Amethyst	"Gabriel"
	"In Quest of the Holy Grail"
Scarlet Leaf Review	"The Beginning and the End"

Talking to God

I throw myself down in my chamber, and I call in, and invite God, and his Angels thither, and when they are there, I neglect God and his Angels, for the noise of a fly, for the rattling of a coach, for the whining of a door.

—John Donne

THE POTTER

I have known the fresh ball of clay,
the slap of it on the wheel,
thumbs opening the turning mouth
and the careful rising
of the fragile walls.

Without my knowing it,
I was imitating You, my Lord
when You created me,
first in the womb, then on my feet
learning to walk like the Son of Man.

I ask that You forgive my collapses,
for I am only mud
and I know nothing.
Be patient with me
that I may serve You as a pitcher.

MESSIAH

Each year we wait for You to join us in
our Seder meal with empty chair for You,
or at festivities like Easter, Christmas.

Are we to live in expectation, daily
examining in moral mirrors if
our peccadilloes, unregarded, make
us too unworthy to behold your face?

For careful as we try to be, we err
unconsciously or else through habit.

We long for justice and for peace of course,
but mercy too. Come help us holy One.
Defend your people with your strength or tact.

NOTHING IN EXCESS

In me You may observe that age
of nations which revert again to tribes.

This is the era of a dagger in
the chest of neighbors who will differ some
in their idea of a perfect world;
the era also of a ton of hatred
to an ounce of care; hatred toward
concession for the blue types or the red.
It is the time extremes are taken as
a form of strength and rally-flag's allure.

Attend my plea, O Lord. It is for me
as much as for my wayward countrymen.
I would be healed of this distrustfulness.
Don't let my will exaggerate the rules
You handed down until they merge with sin.

HIS FOOLISH AIM

My Lord I've sinned most grievously
in seeking the applause of giddy folk
instead of yours.

And when acclaim has come unsought
I strewed the word around as if
it pleased You too.

This tarnished urge to be admired
controlled me when I wore short pants
and has till now.

I search for my excuse in vain
for I have known for years what You
desire from me.

Yet on I went the way a child
is anxious that the world should crave
his new cap-gun.

Is it too late now to repent,
or is that why I've lived so long?
Have mercy Lord.

PRAYER FOR PAIN

Bring on more pain, good Lord,
for as of yet my worst is just one woe.
There is much more, I know,
but still for now I think I can afford

the worst there is to shake
me from nightmares to love your word.
And when it's done, "Absurd"
I'll say of all my woes that then seem cake.

Why do we pray to you
for health? So we'll forsake our beds and walk?
It's just our way to talk
when we are only bored or feeling blue.

FOR THE CHURCH UNIVERSAL

To the Being beyond all being,
the Headwaters of life's moving river,
the Master of time and space:

We who struggle to know You better
in order to love You better
are conscious of this world's
unavoidable tarnishing
of beauty's perfection.

We who trip over tree roots
are lifted to our feet again
by your staff reaching down,
and by your voice, something greater
than a mere vibration of the air,
more than honey to light our eyes.

It is ourselves, each of us remade
at your mouth and breathed into us,
a newborn spirit,
a soul made young again.

Rejuvenator of the world,
make your church new again
as You have remade our lives.
Let it be to us a home,
a cabin in the wilderness
stocked with food and firewood
for travelers adrift like us.

IS THERE ONLY ONE?

Give us the wisdom to decide, good Lord:
Was the Reformation made by You?
Was it to help us find a proper church?
Those of us, I mean, who want to worship
You instead of church? Were these divisions
planned to give us options that might suit
our personalities and predilections
now that we're not so fit for monarchy?

They seem to be, but *seems* may not be truth.
There certainly is greater chance these days
for putting certain churches by, and choosing
one or two that let a Christian love
a neighbor with *agape's* loving care
because both live in awe of You, our God.

Or was Augustine right in thinking one
lone church brought efficacious grace to us?
Or did the man think it because there was
one church that made good sense in his own time?

Allow these questions, Lord, and be not peeved
by our confusions. Guide us by your Spirit
to obey your Son and all be one.
It's clear, however good beginnings are,
that humans will corrupt an institution.

Dramatic Monologues

> The dramatic monologue is a literary form in which the poet takes on the voice of a character and speaks through that character. The term most frequently refers to a poem in which the poet creates a character who speaks without interruption.
> —*A Book of Poetic Forms*

MALCHUS

John 18:10

They said it would be simple.
Help a group of weaponed men
arrest an unarmed man,
keeping eyes and ears
open for reporting to the high priest.
Why would I expect to lose an ear?

I was the only casualty.
Here's the blood I shed,
now dried on my tunic.
It didn't hurt until we found the ear
and stuck it back where it belonged.

Oh my head. I can still feel it cringe,
especially when I'm in bed and roll over.
My fellow captives called me a coward
when I surrendered to the Jews.
This is their lesson.
I was the only casualty.

THE MAGI

Nothing is true below the moon;
only the stars are wise.
That's why we blink at things of earth,
searching the steady skies.

When we observed the rising star,
each from his proper land,
each of us took a mount and food,
met as if all were planned.

On went the star, and we went on
following where it led.
Give no belief to those who say
truth will elude the head.

We had no sense where that child lay;
all we pursued was truth.
Then we were there and found our goal
lodged in a kind of booth.

Down we dismounted, knelt and gave
frankincense, gold and myrrh.
Herod requested we report
but we did not concur.

All three returned to our dear ones,
watching the starlit sky,
all of us changed by what we'd seen.
We now search till we die.

You who are wise and find God's Son,
give more than gifts you bring.
Give every moment, every breath.
Follow Him as your King.

GABRIEL

The Father sent me so of course I went.
The planet and the village both were small.
I was to tell her of the Lord's intent
to mitigate the sickness of the Fall.

I saw her praying, and she seemed to me
an ordinary, not-so-pretty girl.
But when she spoke she seemed an almond tree
about the time its tender blooms unfurl.

When I'd arrived, I was to say, "Fear not."
But when I'd had my say, she looked at me
with eyes that held me rooted to the spot.
"I am a leaf," she said. "He is the sea."

Amazed by these few words, I took my leave,
and marveled how the Father knew his child.
Yet, curious, I hung about the eave
to see her candor. Then she knelt and smiled.

SEEN FROM A CABOOSE

I'm on a train
in its caboose
and looking back
on where I've been.

My past recedes
with all its flaws,
but I'm aware
that my "pure" life
is only due
to His reply.

I'd begged that He
forestall my urge
to break my vows.

He did, but I
retained one flaw
behind the door
that He had locked.

And now I beg
that He remove
my waywardness.
For this jailed flaw
was counterfeit
for life with Him.

The iron wheels
clank with our speed.

My past recedes
with all its wrongs,
and then I sleep
and dream of awe.

SIMON OF CYRENE

How was I to comprehend our roads
would intersect? I had been pleased at my
good fortune on this journey. No robbers
interfered to mar the days I ambled on.

And then when I was almost at the city
a pair of Roman soldiers muscled me
to their will, which was to carry up a hill
the cross a weakened man released and fell.

I, a man of status and of wealth at home,
to act the role of criminal, the shame
that clings to those whom crucifixion suits!
How had I offended YHWH? How?

Cyrene was respected by our race
there in Jerusalem, walled about
with several synagogues for major prayers.
But no man disobeys the Romans' swords.

I took the cross, then took the spittle of
those newcomers who thought I'd earned the role.
Enough! I was not crucified, but bore
the sting of ignominy all that day.

Too old to walk there now, I dream of Him,
his face in blood, his back in rivulets.
The sign above Him said, "Jesus of Nazareth,
king of the Jews." It gives me troubled dreams.

PARABLE FOR OUR TIME

The Father worked to build an edifice
that housed a massive family.
But when the kinfolk came they spurned his plan,
though just a few obeyed his rules.

And from these few He chose a Paragon
to show them love and who He was.
Some of them watched and listened, but the rest
were angered, tortured him; He died.

But like the moon, death lasted just three days.
His Father gestured him to life.
And that was prompt enough to turn a large
proportion to respond with awe.

A PIVOT POINT

If Abelard was right
and Bernard wrong,
we are not saved by
the Crucifixion of Christ,
but by our imitating
His path to the cross.

Can we say when we die
that we have always
taught the truth,
helped to heal, provided
food for the hungry, lived
inwardly as we lived
outwardly, and then
gave up ourselves
to the Father's will,
be it painful or comforting?

But this is only our path
if Abelard was right
and Bernard was wrong.

THE BUSINESS OF REPENTANCE

the Redeemer answers a question

My Father forgives easily.

When a boy fired his slingshot
at a cat in a basket,

or a girl damaged someone's reputation,
or a child stole peaches from a tree
and threw them at sparrows,

all I had to do was
bring that child home
and Father would receive that offspring
as his own.

Of course I never brought home
a child who persisted in
nefarious ways
after promises of reformation.

FANTASTIC SINS

I'm always fantasizing something.
Usually it's about torturing my rapist.

But yesterday I wondered if
merely thinking these is a sin,
so I went to confession where the priest said,
"They are indeed sinful, for as Jesus said
those who merely think of sinning
have sinned in their heart.
Now go and repent, for you have sinned
against God who created your rapist
and is still trying to make him a better man."

So I repented, and my fantasies stopped.
Later on I testified at my rapist's trial
citing only the truth without exaggerating.

I am sending this to your mind from my
hovel on the outskirts of Paradise where
I am grateful to that priest. And to God.

JOSES

Yes of course he was my brother,
or at least our mother was the same.
He was our eldest, and took up
our father Joseph's trade at first.
But when he was, oh I don't know,
thirty I suppose, he paced the road
following our cousin John.

Then Herod took John's head (some
fuss about a dancing girl) and Jesus filled
John's place. He'd always had a knack
for doing what I thought were magic
tricks, but now he seemed to heal some
hopeless cases—a man born blind
I think there was, a woman with a
lifetime flow of blood, the dead
daughter of someone or other.

These accounts trickled home to us,
and James was angered when they did.
Mother wept in silence. The Sadducees
arrested him, and in the end they
killed him on a Roman cross.
Some said he revived and ate
some fish. It would be Jesus' style.

A Miscellany

Accomplished men of letters, such as Julius Vestinus and Aelius Dionysius, selected from his writings choice passages for declamation or perusal, of which fragments are incorporated in the miscellany of Photius and the lexicons of Harpocration, Pollux and Suidas."

—Anonymous

UNSEEN, DR. JOHNSON HEARS PRAISE

Walter Harte once dined with Mr. Cave,
and Harte, who'd read Johnson's "Life of Savage,"
declared the excellence of what he'd read
in several superlatives at once.

On meeting Harte again, Cave told the man
that he had made a certain person happy
when last they'd dined. Johnson, in penury,
had sat behind a screen in shabby clothes.

Something says that there's another setting;
Someone unseen overhearing praise
for something wonderful He had done,
unseen because to see his beauty would be fatal.

DISCOUNTING TRUTHS

Some say that past the ocean there are other
continents. To think such things is not difficult
for we cannot sail very far into the ocean.
—Seneca the Elder, c. 55 BC—AD 37 [/EPI]

How many ideas there are that we suspect
are figments of someone's roiling imagination.

It took *homo sapiens*
millions of years to believe
that germs exist,
that we are on a whirling planet
and yet are not thrown off,
that our sun is only another star
with the benefit of proximity.

And Seneca, were he alive today,
would have brushed aside the factual idea
that the universe was fine tuned at
the Big Bang by the only Mind
existing before that sudden explosion
of space and matter.

THE BEGINNING AND THE END

When the Prime Mover let it be known
that *homo erectus* was his sapient aim,
an angelic committee voiced a moan,
urging that He, the world's Maker, disclaim
this late averment, hinting it would taint
the universe without some taut restraint.

But the Omniscient would have none of it,
so loosed his wisdom unassailable
that the sole redeemer from the pit
be *agape* for himself, and amiable.
Thus were the jealous messengers abashed.
Satan grew his tail; his teeth he gnashed.

Our Earth obeyed its Master: in the oceans,
where gases vented from the floor, fish
fed on them, transitioning through the eons
to seals and apes, obeying the Father's wish.
(This intricate, entangled process grants
dubious sway to miscreants.)

The planet then acquired a race ensouled
who scoured their knowledge to determine why
omnipotence with benignity should scold
his offspring with ruin as if He wished they'd die.
They had scant means to see it was to test
whether their faith was worthy to be blest.

Now in our day a moiety has failed
the test, yet still maintain they've qualified.
And so "the son of perdition," who regaled
himself above the Lord, is pert and snide,
proclaiming he's superior to law,
for he'd invented lies to quell and awe.

The promised end has seemed at sundry times
to gesture its approach, yet stars remained,
though nations quaked. Perhaps, as pantomimes,
they shook the Ninevites, who then regained
their faith. So goes relationship with God,
who will not, like the pagan Zeus, nod.

IN QUEST OF THE HOLY GRAIL

The carmine liquid gleams in shallow cracks.
A few collect it, find it sweet, then sour,
then realize that it has kissed their brains
and made them more alert to minds of light.

But soon an institution forms to keep
this lifeblood as a regulated drink,
a necessary structure in a world
where felons bleed themselves, their servants or
their pigs, and sell it on the road in jars.
It's then the royal blood sinks out of sight,
a memory revered, no longer known.

How to manipulate the world (without
reshaping what we are) to bring it back,
the same old rural scenery of brooks
and holy people in their laundered wool
imbibing simple life from heaven's wells?
How shall we hold our tongues to speak aright;
or cross our fingers, toes or eyes to snare
this sacred cup we somehow cast aside?

OUR ROAD

What massive mind
could there have been
before plain time
and space began?

Why it would care
for wayward lives
when all was peace
I just might know.

Make a round cage.
Let DNA
sublime and drift
to plants, livestock.

Make known the best,
but leave to them
the final choice—
to die or live.

This sifting plan
is our abode.
It's clear we can
choose best our road.

AN OLD STORY

You've heard this all before. Did you forget?
A small and hidden village was destroyed
by vandals, but a few escaped, survived,
and traveled under cover of the night.
For years they lived on roots, mushrooms and grubs.

One day they saw a large tree trembling. Then
it disappeared into the air. The sun
went bright as if someone had turned it on.
We see by light, but this light blinded them
for several days. But soon they saw again.
And then a voice, as if a man should stand
nearby. It said things I must not repeat.
But what it said transformed these few so that
they never traveled in the dark again.

They told their friends, but they would not believe.
They told their children, who had never been
afraid to travel openly. And as the world
grew tamer and more comforting, some took
the words as mere vibrations of the air,
or blackened tracks across a freckled page.

A few would gather weekly after dawn,
but more to be with other saddened souls
than to recall what happened long ago
to those whose life and mind seemed odd to them.
Besides, it was too old to be of use.

Yet all occurred: the vandals and the tree,
the blinding sun, the words somebody spoke,
the dawning age of living in the light.
And if they still remain (why should they not?),
to lose the story would be sheer insanity.

FINGERPRINTS

Our elders one day turned a city corner
and are out of sight.
Even those our age
no longer hear the telephone and pick it up.

Those pubescent friends who thought like us
now cannot think at all
but follow mountebanks,
sell out and wait for comets on a barren hill.

Belief in order fades away, chaos seems god,
and this when science tracks
the fingerprints of God
that seem to prove our Maker built our crib.

DEDICATIONS

Some would like to live a life
that's independent of all laws,
a life with "equalizers" on
the hips of manly men who cuss,
chew tobacco, cheat at cards.

Others want the time to come
when one lone pill will give
an everlasting life of bliss
without the pain of birth or work,
with no regrets or stumbling blocks.

But Someone thought a better way to live
is to accommodate the ways of earth,
the gravity of loss and holding down,
appreciation for the modes of things
and for the hardships of the hard of heart.
But most of all, to use our gifts to heal
those who despair, for we despaired once too.

EASTER

What can be said when we have trudged across
a stony desert, boulders everywhere,
stumbling for what seemed a million years?

What can be said when one man joins our group
(a man not one of us could recognize)
and walked with us awhile, then showed us how
to open boulders, step inside, and find
a dining room, the places set, a host
we finally remember as the one
who showed us how to die and not to die?

When such impossibilities occur
mere words fade like the moon by morning's light.

EASTER II

April is the kindest month,
edging us toward the sun
that Tutankhamen worshiped till
he died and his Egyptians turned
again to old demanding gods.

The Son of Man was truly dead
but rose again, disfigured by
the Roman scourges so that He
was recognized by voice alone.
But it was He who stood and spoke.

The earth is but a mirror of
that grand resurgence of his life,
the peonies and lilies, eggs
resembling rocks but holding chicks
that will this summer lay more eggs.

EASTER SUNDAY

How odd for one to truly die, and then
to live again, to walk and talk, eat fish,
pass through locked doors, invite a skeptic
to touch the holes in hands and feet.

And this two thousand years before sci-fi.
You say the early church concocted it?
So why did they entice embarrassment
by saying many failed to know it's him
until he spoke, or broke the bread for them,
or fed them breakfast fish upon a beach?

Doubting Thomases abound today
because their lives contained no oddness,
or failing that, they have forgotten it.
Only seeds and tubers will die down
to sprout again in spring, to live and bloom.
It's all a matter of what some wish not to see.

SWEET ARE THE USES...

When *homo sapiens* goes for a walk,
he swings his arms in imitation of
his distant quadrupedal ancestor,
that small and agile brute descended from
arboreal delights that died away.

And since then climbing cities have immersed
themselves in seas, diseases have consumed
the moiety of all who speak and write.

What seed is tucked in such adversities
that strikes a root in barren land and holds
its leaves in sunlight as a pact with God?
Is it the usual contrivance of
paternal love that only will chastise
when punishment may carry blessings too?

UNWORTHY

Surrounded by this park of wooded land,
a loving wife, a brilliant son, a noble dog
agreeing with my every gesture and my word,
I am embarrassed by my unearned bliss.

When did I feel a studded whip
or haul uphill the mechanism of my death?
The smallest sacred act, persuading one
to follow Christ, I stumbled and I botched.

And yet I feel his hand that wills me on . . .
to what? The crudest dwelling heaven owns?
My thanks would overflow, and I would stand
attentive to the slightest sign He makes.

For I've done nothing to attract his eye
except to laze away my life and preachify.

LOOKING FOR HEAVEN

Some will read accounts of the cenobitic life,
envisioning thereby small pools of tranquility
hidden from a world of salesmanship, competition,
family arguments at the dinner table,
erotic predation, king-of-the-hill games,
loves focused on everything but God.

We long then to put on the robe of near-equality,
to be addressed as Sister This or Brother That,
to be freed of distractions, to be allowed to pray
unceasingly—one long life of prostration.

But even if it were the heaven we wished,
we still would have to become used to it,
fighting our egos down time after time,
doing battle with our lusts, our appetites
for surprises, our demands for signs from God.

Heaven, as the Man said, is in us,
just waiting for the Sculptor to chip away
everything in us that was not breathed into.

A CHANGE FOR THE BETTER

I told myself I didn't care about
salvation, for loving God was everything.
If He decided I was not enough
to bother with, I would agree with Him.

Who befriends someone because they have
great wealth or influence or think us fine?
It would betray a grasping deviousness
in us and would then fizzle in effect.

But I discovered in my love a wish
to be with Him, the Fountain of all good,
all beauty, clemency and understanding.

And so now I try (how fine it is)
to merge the two, my admiration and
my need to be with Him, the perfect One.

PRAYING OR PLAYING?

When I have fallen out of love with time,
my food like water from a stagnant pond,
my taste for poetry gone dull or nil,
and my delights diminished less than slime,

I think of Him from whom I've had reply.
But none today. None, although I've cast myself
prostrate and begged of Him new life for me.
"Ah, now I see. It is an empty sky."

But no. When He sojourned with us, He died
with arms spread wide as if He would embrace
us all, those downcast or those dignified.

My abject body did not worship Him.
I was an actor begging for belief,
so praying for myself was weak and dim.

AT THE CRUCIAL POINT

As caring parents hold their toddlers' hands
while teaching them to walk as humans do,
and in the course of time they take away
that extra help and let them walk the way
a person does with small aid from above;

so does that careful Father in our lives
facilitate our harder lessons in
maturing souls, until we reach our cross
on which our faith has gained the strength to ask,
"Father, why have You abandoned me?"

For who would so appeal if cast away?

CIVILIZATION

Those who are human and humane;
who love a place and there remain;

who recognize the beauty in
gorilla's stare, the fish's fin,
in running horse, the striding cat,
are kind to canines and the bat;

who can discuss ideas with
a sense of knowledge and of myth
without the competition of
a taste of winning, but of love;

who see injustice and recoil
as they would from some useless toil;

dispensing mercy when in charge
of someone mostly innocent
and set the one accused at large,
especially if they repent—

are truly civilized at heart
and worthy to be set apart.

The Pelegrin Papers

A Set of Narratives

The individual to whom God gave an author's pen must write of the acts of God and his wonders with human beings.

—S. Y. Agnon

1. SIR PELEGRIN

When autumn trees are at their drowsy best,
and geese take to the sky in chatting vees,
old men look back upon their lives and think
they'd like to add a certain thing to what
they said or did, or didn't say or do.

Such did Sir Pelegrin, or I should say
Père Pelegrin, for he had stowed his sword
and armor in the abbey's stables when
he was a novice. Then, years on, ordained,
he'd prayed prostrate along the earthen floor
that his misdeeds be shriven (though he had
adhered to church tradition and confessed
to Père Crèvecoeur), his misdeeds having been
a strict enforcement of the law of love.
That is to say, he hunted down the thieves
and murderers, adulterers, and most
especially abortionists, and set
his holy blade to winkling out the pus
that pocked the body of the Son of God.

But after thirty years of zeal he saw
no differences. One frozen winter night,
disoriented and downcast, he came
upon a hermit's hut amidst the trees,
was welcomed, fed on gruel, slept the night.
He woke in darkness to a muttering.
The hermit prayed. He prayed that Pelegrin
would see that Christ had come to change the world,
not from the outside first, but from within
the core of humankind, the place where all
decisions have their birth. The holy man
had not been asked for his advice, and so
intended none, but Pelegrin had heard.
At dawn, more gruel, and in gratitude

he split some kindling for the hermit's fire,
then asked directions to an abbey's walls.

And this is where he'd been received and, in
good time, ordained. Here he'd not only prayed
for his own soul, but for the welfare of
the world at large, the rapists, thieves,
and grasping vendors of indulgences.
Though good for him, it seemed a little shy
on application. Then he took his sword
and mail again, for Paul had said to take
on you God's armor; and the sword, in dire
necessity, could stand in for a cross.
He told the scowling prior he could stay
no more, then told the abbot, who said, "Go
with God, my son." And so he scrubbed his steel
until it held no whit of rust, and went.

But where to go? And what to do when there?
His horse eyed him suspiciously for want
of having seen or snuffed him ten long years.
The cinch just made it round the fattened steed.
They rode for days beyond the abbey walls,
then Pelegrin pulled back and halted there
the better to consider his new life.
To kill the murderers and rapists meant
they'd have no offspring, some of whom—at least
a few of whom—might one day be bright saints.
Ergo, to root them out would be the same
as what abortionists had done. And yet
(there always was "and yet") to let them live
amounted to participating in
their murders and their violating maids.
It seemed the tares must grow unweeded till
the interwoven wheat was harvested.
Could nothing—should nothing then be done?

The sheep must feed. What did he have that they
could turn to warming wool? He had his life,
or what was left of it at this late date.
He saw it now. The light began to gleam.
He steered his horse toward it with the sense
that nothing now encumbered his free hand.
But even with his life as price, how much
can one man do? The world was like a field
where battle's aftermath was worse than death.
It writhed and cursed and groaned and leaked its life.
The misery was multiple, and he
was only one, a man who'd mired himself,
then had been raised into a state somewhat
near cleanliness. But if a fish or two
and just a few more loaves of bread could sate
the hunger of five thousand men and just
as many wives or children, with God's touch,
it fostered faith that one lone man could do
what many men together might have done.

He rode on through the dank and leafless wood
and thought where he might stage his last tableau,
when like a man hit by the sky's hard fire,
the thought struck him with such a sudden force
he nearly was unseated from his mount:
It was not his to stage. If God agreed
to use his sacrifice for greater good,
God would supply the altar and the day.
And as that proverb settled in his bones,
Sir Pelegrin relaxed, and went his way,
and waited for the ripening of time.

Three years he wandered, and three years he watched.
The challenges from other knights he saw
as juveniles in want of self-respect.
With repetition, this built up for him
a reputation as the "coward knight."

Most children pelted him, as he rode by,
with clods of soil and taunts that he ignored,
except to wonder if these prankish youths
might reap some benefit from his demise.

In time he felt his armor was too much
protection for an ordinary man,
and he'd decided that was what he was.
He sold the steel and made his way again.
He rode in wool, but wore no clericals.
He sold his horse, gave all the money to
a tumble-down, neglected church whose priest
would show up once each month if he had time.
This was the simple church's happy day;
the priest was there, a little tipsy, with
a gift for several boys. In walked our knight,
who crossed himself and knelt and wept his prayers.
And then, when mass was done, he stopped the priest
and gave him all the silver in his pouch.
The priest stared at the money and recoiled.
Where did a poor man get such wealth as this?

Was giving it to him some sort of trap?
Sir Pelegrin replied with all he was
and all he'd ever been, at which the priest
seemed humored and demanded that he stay.

Sir Pelegrin, in meekness, stayed and prayed
that all would serve the Father's loving will.
Forthwith the priest returned and said that he
had seen the bishop, and his excellence
desired to speak with him. He'd had no time
to ride to where the bishop's lodgings were,
but soon the sheriff was outside the church
with extra horses for the priest and Pelegrin.
They rode that afternoon and into night,
then slept but briefly and arrived at noon.
The priest went in, his hair new-combed, and soon

returned to say the bishop would grant him
an audience that evening. That was all.
The knight had long ago renounced his vows,
so owed the prelate nothing legally,
but bishops were not men to trifle with.

When evening came, there were still more delays.
But finally a sallow deacon rang
a trio of small bells, and all three men,
the sheriff, knight and priest, were climbing up
a grand and curving stairway to a room
that seemed afflicted with a pestilence
of putti, naked in cold marble or
in paintings equally disrobed and plump.
Sir Pelegrin could see resemblances
between the priest and bishop, but saw now
that he was in a different diocese.
The sheriff stood outside the door, as if
to hinder Pelegrin's escape. The priest
retold the knight's odd past and begged to know
if ordination and his sudden wealth
might be of service at his excellency's foot.

At this, the knight made bold to say he had
renounced his vows, and even had he not,
he could not in good conscience serve a man
who broke his holy vows of chastity
to lust for little boys. The bishop sneered

and said he felt no need for lowly priests,
defrocked or not, to judge the way he lived.
He'd been ordained as long as most survived
and always kept his tastes restricted to
young men from twelve to seventeen or so.
The sheriff heard this past the door ajar.

A chalice stood upon his writing desk,
and Pelegrin had wondered if the wine
was consecrated. In a blink, the door
crashed open and the bishop's hand swung wide
to steady him, upsetting that which held
what might have been the blood of Christ. The knight
moved like a glance to keep the wine unspilled
as, all unseen, the sheriff's sword struck swift
as any snake and sliced the pilgrim's heart.
This left the bishop's all too shaken one
in safety, to the deep dismay of him
the bishop had molested as a boy,
the sheriff, who had grasped the chance to meet
the bishop once again, and man to man.

So Pelegrin had died, and in his death
had saved a life that voluntarily
disclaimed his bishop's miter to submit
himself as "brother" to an abbot's rule,
as purist applicant for haloed head.
But in a year he came upon despair
and drank a potion that would end his life.
The sheriff, in remorse, soon after lost
his hunger for revenge; the priest appears
for mass more often; and the pious pilgrim
had searched for God's true will for him and found
no certainty until he had been dead.

2. YOUNG PELEGRIN

When Pelegrin was just a tender boy,
his *grand-mère* walked him to her village church,
the same one where the water had been poured
across his brow and back into the font.
Perhaps that leakage caused him to believe
in God instead of church, and back again
to church in place of God, for good or ill.

A bit before his teens he asked his priest
to lay before him how to think of God.
The cleric merely quoted catechism's
cold accretions on belief and life,
then walked away. And so did Pelegrin.

He walked away from incense and the mass,
novenas, and the prayers to saints for men.
And having left behind respect for Rome's
embellished church, he lived a pagan life.

Seducing flocks of simple maids, and feasting
on the labors of the poor, he found
the evanescent thrills gave him no peace.
Seduction was but power over none,
and precious cates were sand upon his tongue.
Therefore he turned ascetic and renounced
the pleasures of those pastries of the world.

No longer did he gaze on shapely girls.
No longer did he eat the flesh of beasts,
but only now and then a bit of fish
augmented by dry barley or some oats,
and washed it down wherever water was,
no matter if it ran or stood in mire.

He wandered weakly, aimlessly, and then
one happy day he spied a castle's turrets.
He begged for entrance. Then, past the drawbridge,
past portcullis, he entreated at
the palace gate for labor as a slave.

But there he served as scullion to the cook,
his wages bits of bread the dogs refused.
A year he worked as hard as starveling could,
when, hearing of his honesty, the lord
commanded that he show his face and speak.
He told his life till then, and his reward
was keeper of the lord's attire. And then
with that success and better food, promotion
to a squire, with daily training from
the knights on horseback and afoot with sword.

When spring suggested ample ale for all,
our Pelegrin was watching dancers step
the carol, when he felt a hand pull
him up to dance. It was a buxom wench,
her face in sweat and glowing from the fire.
And as they danced she puffingly expressed
a wish that he could taste her ale at home.
He blushed, almost accepted, then heard the tone
of her bold words, and pleaded urination's
pressing need. And to the castle he.

Thus did his youthfulness come to an end,
and he became a man, and in due time
a knight, known widely for his hardiness,
and as Sir Pelegrin the paladin.

3. THE SHERIFF

A hundred times I thought about that priest,
his assignations with the village boys.
But then I'd think, "He's not the one who took
advantage of *my* youth." Inane? Of course.
I needed wisdom then to see that I
was not the most important man alive.
Yet still it hampered me from cutting him.

And so I waited for my opening,
a circle I could see around the heart,
the useless heart of that pernicious bishop
through which my sword might find his evil core.

I'd been in awe of him. "Succeeding from
apostles," I'd been told, but never heard
of Peter, James or John molesting boys.
What was the source of this abhorrent plunder
if not the twisted righteousness of hell?

My Jeanette was but eighteen when we
were wed, and I was twenty-one. I wooed
in public till I had her will, and then
besought her father's yes. There was no masked
avoidance, furtive, unrevealable.
I make no boast of this. I only say
mankind must be kept holy and unsoiled.

And so when opportunity allowed
revenge, my sword knew what to do, and would—
or so I thought. My target was, however,
moving quick, and I was guilty of
dispatching one who was without vile sin.

I then examined what I'd done and tossed
my vengeance with confession and repentance
for my scurvy quest. I cannot say
my life since then was sinless every day,
but my besetting search for murder was
cast out, along with office's respect.

Confessions through a cleric unresolved,
I'm left with my petitions for relief.
And while I pray, I pause. That's when I see
that Pelegrin was imitating Christ.
Therefore his death had drawn us close to Christ,
and I, the soldier hammering His nails—
guilt-ridden, or an imperceptive saint?

4. THE DRUNKARD PRIEST

When *Père Ivrogne* overcame his shock,
at how by chance the bishop might have died,
assessing his whole life, he saw two things:
his inclination toward young boys and his
resulting drunkenness. He feared them both
and prayed to Holy Catherine for help.
Then with a prophet's ember on his tongue,
he began to preach what he desired
for himself, a purity of life.

He had no clear idea how he could
bring this about, but when another bishop
took the seat left vacant, he was sent
into another church and told that if
his escapades continued, he would be
defrocked, with all his errors publicized.

Newly placed, he found this church came with
a permanent housekeeper, Beauregard,
a man who could not be disported with.
This sobered him, and in a year he fell
in love with Beau. It was the first and last
time he'd acquired an unsalacious love,
he thought. And Beauregard had come around
to much the same. And so they slept as one.

This handsome man let nothing slip his lips
that was not to the point. But "helpful" was
almost his second name, and this impressed
Ivrogne so, the priest grew fond of him.
But even this disturbed the conscience of
the priest, so when the bishop summoned him
on other matters, he confessed. The bishop
then complained of hearing loss, and told
him to in future come to him for shrift.

So then Ivrogne felt that he moved toward
what heaven asked of him with all his faults.

He was no longer tipsy at the mass,
so dropped the sobriquet in deference
to his birth name, which was Pierre, and said
so from the pulpit when he preached on truth.
Now while his sermon was developing,
he thought, with all the verve of new-found truths,
he ought not keep his new life to himself.
Of course the bishop heard of this. He railed
at Père Pierre for shaming him, defrocked
the priest. He'd be replaced within a week.

Eleven days, and then the man arrived
in courtly dress, pomade within his hair,
and with a fair companion wearing vair
about her wrists and collar. Pierre and his
friend Beauregard were mounted up and gone
as soon as their replacements had arrived.

They'd taken food with them, but soon ran out.
Pierre had brought his knife, his friend his bow.
The life of forester would please them both,
especially since Beau had lived this life
before the bishop hired him to be
housekeeper and companion. So he taught
Pierre to bend the bow and let the arrow
fly into the mark, with minor misses.

On they went until the cold came on.
The hunting had improved, but they had need
of shelter, so they traded flesh for lodging
with a widow haggard-thin and much
in need of flesh. But soon they made it clear
that they were not her kind. Still she kept
them on, for she made up in wisdom what
she lacked in meat. And all the while Pierre

had learned to shoot down flying geese, along
with deer and feral pigs. But something lacked.

On thinking through again his early life,
he realized he'd shed from him all three:
the boys, the wine, and with those two the church.
For he was not the kind of man who could
be satisfied with life without some bones
within the flesh of faith: the liturgy,
the doctrine and a hierarchy for form.
So he proposed to Beauregard that they
store up for their now-plumper hostess meat,
then take their way to church. But Beauregard
accepted none of it, and bade Pierre
God-buy-ye. With a hearty clasp and many

admonitions to be ware, the friends
were parted, and one horse bore one away.

Alone again, but hopeful for all that,
he rode among the springtime wood reciting
Paternoster, Ave Mária
and more. The game evaded him, for he
was bowless now. A partridge mocked him from
the underbrush, but then he heard the chorus
of a forest filled with vernal birds.
It was his first delight in God's creation.

He acquired a bow (I'll not say how)
and later arrows, sold the meat he'd pierced
and with the proceeds bought a better bow,
returning the deficient one. And then,
through grace, he stumbled on a likely friend,
a small and pale adult who saw Pierre's
new faith.

         The friend knew of a church nearby
and diocese that greeted them with clasps.
And there was lacked a sacristan. Pierre
was there and qualified. His friend was bailiff's
scribe, which kept him happily at pen.
The former priest had compromised enough
his lust for boys to satisfy one corner
of the church; then drank in moderation.
The two of them continued as a pair
until the earth had covered both one month.

Pierre thought Pelegrin's demise had helped,
and who am I to say that he was wrong?

5. THE BISHOP

To shrink the little self-respect I had,
the Spaniards have discovered some new world
off to the West. What am I bishop of?
This meager plat, this pygmy principate,
this patch upon the mother church at large.

And now the world is larger than it was,
and my fiefdom insignificant.
This new world teems with heathens we must raise
to heady altitudes of "right belief."
Am I prepared to hear the papal choice
to oversee their transformation, who
once quivered in the presence of adults?

Am I to marshal priests who waver not
confronting bladed savages and tics?
I will confess I own no martial heart.
Me for satin sheets and milky skin.
Me for loving thrust, not sticking steel.
And yet, not lover neither—predator.

I learned eft-times just who the sheriff was
and that we'd met before. It was a blow
that worried me as dogs do rats or cats.
If he was able to insert himself
into my high security, why then
which one of my grown toys will seek me next?

My guardedness invited punishment
for working them to cries and shrieks and tears.
The unseen man sniffed opportunity,
and mere fatality protected me
from hateful death. Divine aversion? No!
A loving god is not about to raise
me to apostleship and then turn coat

to frighten me with momentary shirk.
If god exists, I've always said, he is
of evil and of good in equal parts.

I therefore am resolved to tuck my life
within the walls of monkery where I'll
be fed and bedded, nay respected for
my highest self. I'll implement this plan
upon the morrow and be off, and safe.
But how to rid myself of my remorse?
A pest it is and throwback to my youth.
Ah well, if it should come to that, I'll have
communion wine with potions so I'll "sleep."

6. SIR PELEGRIN'S GRANDDAUGHTER

While Pelegrin went through his pagan phase,
a number of young maidens knew his bed.
On his departure from these wastrel days,
he'd had no inkling that he left behind
a scattering of children, some of whom
survived their childhood and became
a coterie of teens. Some of these boys
and girls were several times affected by
Sir Pelegrin's submission to God's will.
But as for others, one may teach, despite
the fact that actions fade into the past.

A dozen adolescents grew to love
that stirring in their hearts and in their groins.
Eventually, and unawares, a pair
of them succumbed to these. They fell in love,
and also fell in lust so heavily
that nothing served to keep the two apart.
They kissed. (It was a venial sin.)

And then she bore a child, a pretty thing
who suckled, burbled, spat up food, and peed.
Nancy coped somehow at this new life,
insisting they be married at the church's door.
Henri at last agreed, but had small sleep,
what with the baby's nighttime cries. Then he
became abusive, striking Nancy for
her quickening with child and her complaints.

Henri had hated how these things had gone,
so kept his distance by invading other
huts for stealing goods to sell, lodging
finally in jail for burglary,
where jailors called him "bleeder" when red flowed
from him, the aftermath of blows and kicks.

When grudgingly released, he fled apart,
and no one local heard from him at all.

But Nancy raised young Belle by begging at
the doors of neighbors better fed than she,
her daughter on her hip and on her mind.
And there were times, the wife away from home,
that husbands took their comfort from her youth.

One of them molested her until
his wife came home and caught him in the act.
There was an argument, and then a fight
in which she'd beaten him. Recovered, he
determined he would poison her, and did.
In court, he "did not know the mushrooms well,"
was freed, and took young Nancy and her child
to live with him and in effect be slaves,
Nancy for now, and Belle when she grew up.

But Nancy found accommodations worse
than with Henri, and so announced that she
was taking Belle to church to be baptized,
slipped out the door and did not stop until
she reached her mother's home, mulling all
the while step-father's lack of sympathy,
when out the door her mother ran with shouts
of glee, step-father in her wake, all smiles.

The girl grew tall, her mother wiser than
she'd been, and all went well enough until
Henri returned, having heard of Belle,
demanding ownership, a "father's right."
At sixteen years, Belle understood, and soon,
before Henri convinced the older man,
she ran as fast as arrow to some nuns
in walled retreat from marriage and abuse.
They took her in, and soon she was a novice,
then beyond novitiate, a nun.

Henry meanwhile had died the bleeder's death.

In time, she had permission to attend
to lepers in their colony. She bathed
their lips and noses till she caught what their
affliction was and suffered with the sick.
At thirty she was dead of the disease.

Some say St.Pelegrin looked on her with
an eye of love, approval and delight.

7. THE BOY AT THE BISHOP'S PALACE

When Pelegrin was dead, a boy was there
to take the action in and from it grow.

Inside the palace, four grown men convened,
three within the bishop's library,
his Excellency's self, a priest, and knight.
The fourth, a sheriff, stood outside the door,
apparently preventing one's escape,
but truly stood to hear the conversation
of the three within. Behind him, shadowed
by a column, a pubescent boy
stood still as marble that the column held.

The boy could hear the melodies of speech
but not the meanings. Nearer though, the man
absorbed and understood it all. He heard
the knight face down the bishop. Then the bishop,
in his own defense, unwittingly
admitted to affairs with beardless boys.

This struck the sheriff's anger past his poise.
He slammed aside the door and leaped on through,
his sword blinked from its sheath, and expertly
he aimed at the soiled heart episcopal.

But in the self-same instant as his thrust,
the knight stepped in to save what might have been
some consecrated wine, the blood of Christ;
and in so doing, crossed the sword's bright path,
so took it in his own hale heart instead.

And in the doorway stood the boy, René,
who saw it all unfold. He stared in shock
to see the knight fall heavy to the floor,
hear the sheriff shout, the bishop shriek.

He'd known the like when pigs were slaughtered
for their flesh and blood, but not of man.
It lived within his mind the rest of his
brief life, and came to him with common shrieks,
or in the night when owls were wide awake.
Then all was sorted, Pelegrin to grave,
the sheriff stripped of office, and to ensuing
life as monk the bishop went. René
was brought to priory while commoners
spoke of the knight's quick death as sacrifice.

And then the boy lived on with wholesome work
in field with grain and kitchen garden turnips,
planting seed, then harvesting to share
produce with all, made filling with an egg.

His visions came at opportune occasions,
at silent meals when some monk read Christ's death.
He began to see the knight's unplotted death
had freed him of abuse, and might have been
an act of Providence, true sacrifice,
which in the passing years intrigued him so
that he requested leave to roam the world
while seeking God's own will for him at last.

He died at twenty-five, a married man,
defending wife from Norman ravagers.

www.ingramcontent.com/pod-product-compliance
Lightning Source LLC
Chambersburg PA
CBHW071742040426
42446CB00012B/2445